Native American Civil Rights

Indian Exemptions and Entrepreneurship

Rudy James

INTRODUCTION

If you are the descendants of any of the indigenous peoples of the Americas on either side of your family this book is for you.

Many laws, treaties, agreements and pacts have been written in your favor that you've never been told about.

You have the possibility of living tax-free no matter what your endeavor.

Think about it! No withholding, sales tax, property tax, etc… What if you'd like to start a business? Think how you could prosper if you were to start a tax-free lumber company, car lot, retail store, etc., anywhere you choose (this tax-free status is yours wherever you go). This means all the taxes attached to the products you buy for resale must be subtracted before you pay.

Do you think you could make a go of it if you could charge 30% less and still make a profit? Another benefit is that you don't have to collect taxes for or report to anyone. That means your business records don't have to be shown to anyone. Since your properties don't have to be on tax roles you can actually own them free of Federal, State or local interference rather than just be a title holder. They are not part political country where they lie.

Mr. Damon Marturion

CONTENTS

ACKNOWLEDGMENTS

I owe certain individuals who have assisted and aided me in developing this very specific work on Laws for the Indigenous (Native Americans), Peoples and Nations. Mr. Carl Bern for providing a dwelling while I worked on this project, Mr. Jack McCloud for his support, input, and encouragement, and Mr. Milo Nelson who gave invaluable advice on legal matters and technical advice.

For the two lovely Ladies who kindly rendered their typing skills but requested that their names not be used in the acknowledgements section, thanks for your considerable time and effort.

1. INTRODUCTORY REMARKS

I take this opportunity to express my sincere and deep thanks for being able to share this important information with those who want to improve and safeguard their people. We of the United Indigenous Nations (UIN) have done many years of legal research to gather together pertinent information and legal documents that dramatically impact our Indigenous Peoples and nations.

Many of you have the resolve to continue as a Nation and to preserve your independence and sovereignty. It is truly inspiring to know that some of your Leaders are determined to seek solutions to your problems. Like my Thlingit Peoples, you owned your lands long before the United States of America, Canada, or the Nations of South and Central America came into being. We are here to support you in your efforts of self-determination. The Kuiu Kwaan, the United Indigenous Nations, and the International Human Rights Association of American Minorities support your efforts to preserve your Identity as a people. We support your right to exercise your sovereignty over your territories, your resources, and your people.

We have studied Tribal, Common, and International Law, and Federal statutes for many years. It is amazing how many of these laws recognize the Inherent Rights of the Indigenous Peoples and Nations. Native Americans have not been utilizing those tools and mechanisms for our Indigenous Peoples. Many reasons have been suggested why this is so, such as:

- There are government agencies, corporate entities, and other individuals that are aware about these favorable laws for Indigenous Peoples and have been keeping them secret to keep us in the dark.

- They conspire to keep us in a hopeless and helpless state in order to control us and access our vast resources.

- Their desire is to take complete control over everything that our forefathers maintained, and sometimes fought and died for.

- These immigrant powers and authorities want us to forget who we are and to absorb us into their immigrant societies.

- The backbone of their plan is to keep us divided and fighting with each other, ignore our problems and to do away with us.

- Another is to keep us tied to their financial apron strings and to give us just enough support and financial assistance to keep us dependent on them, but not enough for us to prosper.

- These immigrant organizations and agencies are whittling away on the reservation lands, waters and resources. Some reservations have lost control of over 90% of their lands to non-Tribal members. Please be aware that we know legal methods to have those lands and resources returned.

- Immigrant courts have jailed a high percentage of our Indigenous men, women and youth and turned our people into a "cash crop" that keeps many non-Indigenous persons employed through many times bogus criminal prosecutions and difficult parole programs. We know how to reopen those cases and place those people under our jurisdiction.

- In some geographical regions of this continent the immigrant authorities have denied the Indigenous Peoples access to their traditional foods, medicines, ceremonial objects and their traditional way of making a living.

- The immigrant peoples have used fraudulent, illegal methods and means to appropriate to themselves much of our lands, waters, and resources.
  - o Many of our Indigenous Nations have vast wealth in mineral resources that are not being utilized for the benefit of the Allodial Title Holders, who are our Peoples.

- There exist legal avenues available that can correct and reverse many, if not all, the illegal actions that our People have needlessly endured. We invite you to become completely familiar with the information that we are sharing. Traditional Tribal Leaders who truly love and honor their People will take positive steps to protect and ensure their Peoples' continuation.

This definitive book has compiled all of the pertinent information necessary to understand how individual Native Americans and their nations may interface peacefully with any other peoples and nations of the world. The contents of this book are based on law.

RUDY JAMES

2 SOVEREIGNTY

What is Sovereignty?

- A Sovereign Nation, politically speaking, is equal to any Nation of the world!

- The citizens of an Indigenous Nation are beholden to their own Laws, Rules, Regulations, Ordinances, Loyalty, Personal Behavior, and the Indigenous Nation exercise Personal Jurisdiction over their citizens where ever they reside.

- Sovereigns are the complete and final authority over all that is theirs.

- Complete independence! Sovereigns do not seek permission for their personal actions and deeds from any entity.

- A Sovereign Nation can and must have their own Courts and Judicial System (a nation having its own courts and legal system is the finest way to protect itself and its citizens.)

- Present day Sovereigns are not beholden to any agreement that was made in earlier times by their ancestors who basically did not speak or write the English language.
  - Special Note; All Treaties, Agreements and understandings are subject to detailed and focused scrutiny.

- Everything between Nations is reciprocal.

- The first citizenship of a Sovereign Indigenous person belongs to his/her Indigenous Nation. An Indigenous person can and may have several citizenships.

- A Sovereign Nation can make a treaty, agreement, understanding, a compact, a trade agreement with any Nation (s),

- A Sovereign Nation can make Laws, Rules, Regulations, Ordinances, Licenses, for their citizens,

The foregoing are some of what it means to be Sovereign. These are some of the main things, however it is not all the Sovereignty points.

3 CHOICES

We All Have Choices

Especially Native Americans!

- There are many Laws in our favor that are now in force and very few people are going to tell you about these laws and what they really mean.

- These laws come from;

  o International Treaties,
  o Accords,
  o Understandings and Agreements,
  o United Nation Laws,
  o U.S. Federal Laws,
  o Court Decisions,
  o Traditional Tribal Law,
  o Common Law.
  o Court Action

By using these Laws we can;

- Have true justice by having our own Judicial System with our own Traditional Tribal Courts (and never be brought before any court except our own court.)

- We can start our own businesses that are completely tax free and never have to collect taxes for any entity except our own Traditional Tribal Government.

- The things that we own can never be taxed like our income, properties, houses and lands, etc. by any municipal, county, state or federal agency.

- We can have our own driver's licenses, Insurance Companies, Passports, etc.

- We can be completely Self-Sufficient in all things and we can be free to harvest and use our own medicines as well as utilizing modern medicine.

- We can have Hunting and Fishing Rights and Harvest from Nature and practice all the things our Ancestors did generations ago!

All these good things are ours! But it will not happen without us doing some hard work. If you truly love your family and People do something! This is what these documents are about! We Indigenous People can make it happen.

Native Americans can be Sovereign!

This Should Be the Goal of All Indian Nations and Peoples

To be Sovereign means that the Indigenous Tribes, Nations and Peoples have the same Rights and privileges as any other Nation on earth. They can exercise and practice in ways that are not available to any other individual groups of people in the USA. Sovereign people are completely their own authority and boss. They are able to act completely independent and can negotiate with whomever they choose. To be Sovereign is similar to being the head of a household, except this is done on a national basis. Sovereign means ruler. You are an independent authority over your own domain.

4 UNITED STATES LAW

There are numerous laws that describe and establish the SOVEREIGN RIGHTS OF THE Indigenous (Peoples) and Nations of North America. The following legal citations are just a partial list of some of those Rights.

Laws from THE UNITED STATES OF AMERICA:

The Northwest Ordinance of 1787

"(1 Stat. 50) Article 3 assured that "The utmost faith shall always be observed towards the Indians; their lands and property shall never be invaded or disturbed, unless in just and lawful wars authorized by Congress; but laws founded in justice and humanity, shall from time to time be made for preventing wrongs being done to them, and for preserving peace and friendship with them."

The Indian Tribal Justice Act

EXPCITE – TITLE 25 – INDIANS CHAPTER 38 – INDIAN TRIBAL JUSTICE SUPPORT, Sec. 3601. Findings – STATUTE "The Congress finds and declares that –

(1)   "there is a government-to-government relationship between the United States and each Indian tribe;"

(2) "the United States has a trust responsibility to each tribal government that include the protection of the sovereignty of each tribal government;"

(3) "Congress, through statues, treaties, and the exercise of administrative authorities, has recognized the self-determination, self-reliance, and inherent sovereignty of Indian tribes;"

(4) "Indian tribes possess the inherent authority to establish their own form of government, including tribal justice systems;"

Senate Congressional Resolution 76

100TH Congress, First Session
IN THE SENATE OF THE UNITED STATES

September 16, 1987

AIR. INOUYE for himself), MR. EVANS, MR. DECONCINI. MR. VERDICT, all Mr. MCCAIN. MR. ADAMS. MR. MORAN, MR. CONRAD, MR. HANSEN, MR. D, AMATO, MR. DOLE, MR. FORD, MR. FOLLOWER, MR. THAT the, MR. PAL, MR. RYER, MR. REID, MR. RIEGLE, and this MR. STAFFORD), submitted the following: current resolution; which was referred to the Select Committee on Indian Affairs.

CONCURRENT RESOLUTION

To acknowledge the contribution of the Iroquois off Confederacy of Nations to the development of the United States Constitution and to reaffirm the continuing government-to-government relationship between Indian tribes and the United States established in the Constitution.

Whereas the original framers of the Constitution, including most notably, George Washington and Benjamin Franklin, are known to have greatly admired the concepts, principles and governmental practices of Six Nations of the Iroquois Confederacy; and

Whereas the Confederation of the original Thirteen Colonies into one Republic was explicitly modeled upon the Iroquois Confederacy as were many of the democratic principles which were incorporated into the Constitution itself; and,

Whereas since the formation of the United States, the Congress has recognized the sovereign status of Indian tribes, and has, through the exercise the powers reserved to the Federal Government in the Commerce Clause of the Constitution (art.1 sec. cl. Three), dealt with Indian tribes on a government-to-government basis and has, through the treaty clause (art.11, s2, cl 2) entered into 370 treaties with Indian tribal nations; and,

Whereas of the first treaty entered into with an Indian nation. The treaty with the Delaware Indians on September 17, 1778. And thereafter in every Indian treaty until the cessation by treaty making in 1871, the Congress has assumed a trust responsibility and obligation to the Indian tribes, and their members to "exercise the utmost good faith in dealings with the Indians" as provided for in the Northwest Ordinance of 1787, (1 Stat.50); and,

Whereas Congress has consistently reaffirmed these fundamental policies over the past two-hundred years through legislation specifically designed to honor this special relationship; and (House of Representatives concurring),

- the Congress, on the occasion of the two-hundredth anniversary of the signing of the United States Constitution, acknowledges the historical debt which this, Republic of the United States America owes to the Iroquois Confederacy and other Indian nations for their demonstrations of enlightened, democratic principles of government an example of a free association of independent Indian nations;

- the Congress also hereby reaffirms the constitutionally recognized government-two-government relationship with the Indian tribes which has historically been the cornerstone of this Nations official Indian policy;

- the Congress specifically acknowledges and reaffirms the trust responsibility and obligation of the United States government to Indian tribes, including Alaska natives, for their preservation, and protection and enhancement, including the provision of health, education, social and economic assistance programs as necessary, to assist tribes to perform their government responsibility to provide for the social and economic well-being of their members and to preserve tribal cultural identity and heritage; and

- the Congress also acknowledges the need to exercise the utmost good faith in upholding its treaties with the various tribes, as the tribes understood them to be, and the duty of a great nation to uphold the oldest legal and moral obligations for the benefit of all its citizens so that they and their posterity may also continue to enjoy the rights they have enshrined in the United States Constitution for time immemorial.

Rights of Indians not Impaired; Boundaries

R.S. 1839; Public Law 980213, 15(a), Dec. 8, 1983, 97 Stat. 1462

"Nothing in this Title shall be construed to impair the rights of person or property pertaining to the Indians in any Territory, so long as such rights remain un-extinguished by treaty between the United States and such Indians, or to include any Territory which, by treaty with any Indian tribe, is not, without the consent of such tribe embraced within the territorial limits or jurisdiction of any State or Territory,…"

The Indian Trade and Intercourse Act 1834

Purchases or Grants of Lands from Indians, R.S. was from Act June 30, 1834 (25 U.S.C. ss 177).

"No purchase, grant, lease or other conveyance of lands, or of any title or claim thereto, from any Indian nation or tribe of Indians, shall be of any validity in law or equity, unless the same be made by treaty or convention entered into pursuant to the constitution...."

The U.S. Constitution Supremacy Clause

Article VI, paragraph 2 states:

"This constitution, and the Laws of the United States which shall be made in pursuance thereof; and all Treaties made, or which shall be made, under the Authority of the United States, shall be the Supreme Law of the Land; and the judges in every state shall be shall be bound thereby, anything in the Constitution of the Law of any state to the contrary notwithstanding."

United States Constitution, Article 1, Section 8, Powers of Congress Commerce Clause

"The Congress shall have Power To lay and collect Taxes, Duties, Imposts and Excises, to pay the Debts and provide for the common Defence and general Welfare of the United States; but all Duties, Imposts and Excises shall be uniform throughout the United States..."

United States Constitution, Article 1, Section 8,

"To regulate Commerce with foreign Nations, and among the several States, and with the Indian Tribes..."

United States Constitution, Article XVI, Income Taxes authorized

"The Congress shall have power to lay and collect taxes on incomes, from whatever source derived, without apportionment among the several States, and without regard to any census or enumeration".

Note: An income means an increase. If one trades time for money or goods no income is realized because it was an even trade, just like trading a cow for a horse if both were considered to have equal value.

Public Law 100-606 – Genocide Act Codified

November 4, 1988

"(1) In the case of an offense under subsection (a) (1), a fine of not more than $1,000,000.000   and imprisonment for life; and

(2) a fine of not more than $1,000,000.00 or imprisonment for not more than twenty years, or   both, in any other case."

(c) INCITEMENT OFFENCE –" Whosoever in a circumstance described in subsection (d) directly and publicly incites another to violate subsection (a) shall be fined not more than $500.000 or imprisonment not more than five years, or both."

(d) Required circumstance for offense.

(1)"The offense is committed within the United States

(2) The alleged offender is a national of the United States."

Will v. Michigan Department of State Police

Decided by Supreme Court, ruling reported 1991
491 US. 58, 57 L W 4677 (1989)

State Officials sued in their individual capacities are "persons" under 42 USC 1983 who may be held liable for damages for civil rights violations. State officials can be held personally liable for actions taken in the course of their official duties. Justice Sandra Day O'Connor wrote thus, section 1983 was designed to redress violation of civil rights by persons acting under the color of state law and thus stood the statute on his head to hold that a state official could not be held liable "precisely because of her authority as a state official."

SPERRY OIL and GAS versus CHISHOLM

(264 United States 488), 68 L. Ed. 03. 44 S. CT 372, it was found

"... nor can the state courts assume jurisdiction in a controversy involving Indians."

CONCLUSION

It is abundantly clear that the government of the United States of America considers the Indigenous Nations and Peoples to be a separate People and Nation. Clearly the Indigenous Peoples and Nations are not subject to any form of taxation from any entity, except that of their own. The Indigenous Peoples and Nations have the right to own and operate a business away from their Reservation or "Trust Lands," without business licenses or permits excepting their own. The intention of the Indigenous Peoples and Nations is to own and operate businesses not only on their reservations but also in other areas that are clearly not recognized as Indian Reservations or Trust Lands, all without any form of taxation excepting their own!

Public Law 83-280

(67 Stat. 588, 18 U.S.C. ss 1162 and 28 U.S.C. ss 1360)

Limitation of state authority to alienate tribal land rights:

"(Nothing in this Act authorized the)...alienation, encumbrance or taxation of any real or personal property, including water rights belonging to any Indian or Indian tribe, band, or community that is held in trust by the United States or is subject to a restriction against alienation imposed by the United States; or shall authorize regulation or the use of such property in a manner inconsistent with any federal treaty, agreement or statute or with any regulation made pursuant thereto...."

Cite as PL 83-280, 28 USC 1360 (2001)

(Comment: This act prohibits states from asserting jurisdiction within Tribal boundaries without Tribal consent)

Powers of Indian Tribes Nathan R. Margold

In the opinion of Nathan Margold on Powers of Indian Tribes approved October 25, 1934

(55 I.D. 14):

"It is fact that State governments and administrative officials have frequently trespassed upon the realm of tribal autonomy, presuming to govern the Indian tribes through State law or departmental regulation or arbitrary administrative fiat, but these trespasses have not impaired the vested legal powers of local self-government which have been recognized again and again when these trespasses have been challenged by an Indian tribe."

Superfund Amendments and Reauthorization Acts of 1986

(PL 99-499) The SARA Amendments to the Clean Water Act:

recognize the Indian Tribes as co-trustees of the environment and identify broad powers for chronicling and reporting water resource emergencies, furthermore, testimony from Tribes carries the weight of rebuttable presumption, the term 'Rebuttable Presumption' refers to the fact that a Committee that is formed to closely examine when 'determining losses and restoration' arrives at a dollar figure no governmental agency or political subdivision, even the United States Supreme Court can change that dollar figure and an Indigenous Person can head that said committee along with other individuals (experts), when determining losses and restorations. The Amendments define "Indian tribe" as any Indian tribe, band, and nation or other organized group or community, including any Alaskan Native Village, but not including any Alaskan Native regional or village corporation...Page 5172.

United States v. Winans, 1905
(198 U.S. 371)

"...The U.S. Supreme Court held that the Indians could cross private property to get to their fishing stations. The Supreme Court found that the right to resort to the fishing places in controversy was **a part of larger right possessed by the Indians, upon the exercise of which there was not a shadow of impediment, and which were not much less necessary to the existence of the Indians than the atmosphere they breathed.** New conditions came into existence, to which those rights had to be accommodated. Only a limitation of them, however, was necessary and intended, not taking away. **That is, the treaty was not a grant to the Indians, but a grant from them.**"

The Wheeler-Howard Act of June 18, 1934

(48 Stat. 984-988) As Amended by the Act of May 1, 1936, Section 16:
"...to prevent the sale, disposition, lease or encumbrance of tribal lands, interest in lands, or other tribal assets without the consent of the tribe..."

Wheeler-Howard Disclaimer

Protecting interest in tribal Possessory claims in Section 2 and 15 of the Act (48 Stat. 984-988): (Section 2) (providing)...

Section 150 providing that "...Nothing in this Act shall be construed to impair or prejudice any claim or suit of any Indian Tribe against the United States."

Native Village of Venetie I.R.A. Council vs. Alaska

Adds further understanding and interpretation of the Indian Child Welfare Act, 944 F.2d 548 (9th Cir. 1991) states:

"8. Indians 6(2). In interpreting Indian Child Welfare Act, Congress can be presumed to know that statutes passed for benefit of Indian tribes will be liberally construed in favor of tribes. Indian Child Welfare Act of 1978, S. 2-403, 25 U.S.C.A. S 1901-1963."

"13. Indians 32(1). Indian tribe need not wait for affirmative grant of authority from Congress in order to exercise dominion over its members."

"14. Indians 2. Indian groups to be recognized as sovereign should be those entities which historically acted as bodies politic,..."

Section C. "Alaska errs, however, in seeking to impose upon Indian law doctrines from other fields of law. Because of the unique legal status of Indians in American jurisprudence, legal doctrines often must be viewed from a different perspective from that which would obtain in other areas of law." *See, e.g., White Mountain Apache Tribe v. Bracker*, 448 U.S. 136, 143 100 S. Ct 2578, 2583, 65 L.Ed.2d 665 (1980)

"Statutes are to be construed liberally in favor of the Indians; ambiguous provisions are to be interpreted to the Indians' benefit." Blackfeet Tribe, 471 U.S. at 766, 105 S. Ct. at 2403.

(Comment: Important decision recognizing the fact that Indian Law stands upon Indian Law.)

5 INTERNATIONAL LAW

International Covenant on Civil and Political Rights

Entry into force 23 March 1976, in accordance with Article 49

(Comment) The following cited International Laws have been agreed upon and signed by the United States of America, under the Supremacy Clause of the U.S. A. Constitution these laws become the Supreme Law of the land.

United Nations Law
Preamble

"The States Parties to the present Covenant, Considering that, in accordance with the principles proclaimed in the Charter of the United Nations, recognition of the inherent dignity and of the equal and inalienable rights of all members of the human family is the foundation of freedom, justice and peace in the world,

Recognizing that these rights derive from the inherent dignity of the human person,

Recognizing that, in accordance with the Universal Declaration of Human Rights, the ideal of free human beings enjoying civil and political freedom and freedom from fear and want can only be achieved if conditions are created whereby everyone may enjoy his civil and political rights, as well as his economic, social and cultural rights,

Considering the obligation of States under the Charter of the United Nations to promote universal respect for and observance of, human rights and freedoms,

Realizing that the individual, having duties to other individuals and to the community to which he belongs, is under a responsibility to strive for the promotion and observance of the rights recognized in the present Covenant, Agree upon the following articles:"

PART I
Article 1

(1.) All peoples have the right of self-determination. By virtue of that right they freely determine their political status and freely pursue their economic, social and cultural development."

(2.) All peoples may, for their own ends, freely dispose of their natural wealth and resources without prejudice to any obligations arising out of international economic co-operation, based upon the principle of mutual benefit, and international law. In no case may a people be deprived of its own means of subsistence."

PART III
Article 11

"No one shall be imprisoned merely on the ground of inability to fulfill a contractual obligation."

Article 12

(1.) Everyone lawfully within the territory of a State shall, within that territory, have the right to liberty of movement and freedom to choose his residence."

(2.) Everyone shall be free to leave any country, including his own."

(4.) No one shall be arbitrarily deprived of the right to enter his own country."

Article 17

(1.) No one shall be subjected to arbitrary or unknown interference with his privacy, family, home or correspondence, nor to unlawful attacks on his honour and reputation."

(2.) Everyone has the right to the protection of the law against such interference or attacks."

Article 18

(1.) Everyone shall have the right to freedom of thought, conscience and religion. This right shall include freedom to have or to adopt a religion or belief of his choice, and freedom, either individually or in community with others and in public, or private, to manifest his religion or belief in worship, observance, practice and teaching."

PART VI
Article 50

"The provisions of the present Covenant shall extend to all parts of federal States without any limitations or exceptions."

6 TRADITIONAL TRIBAL LAW

(on Banishment)

Depending on one's personal conduct, any tribal member can be banished from his Tribal Nation. How long depends on an unbiased Court or the involved Tribal Elders.

KUIU KWAAN TRADITIONAL TRIBAL COURT

Declaratory Judgment

THE INHERENT RIGHTS OF THE INDIGENOUS PEOPLE OF NORTH AMERICA

This document is to inform all the Nations of the world of certain irrefutable facts concerning Indigenous People. This factual data recognizes portions of Traditional Tribal Law – United States federal Law – United Nations Law – Common Law – Treaties and Accords and Understandings.

THE KUIU KWAAN THLINGIT NATION

This document is for those Nations that want to make a change. This about an Indigenous government changing to Traditional Tribal Government and Court based on Traditional Tribal Law and some USA federal law and some International Law and some Common Law.

Traditional Tribal Government and Court

All Indigenous governments have a choice to either stay with the Bureau of Indian Affairs Court that are mostly based on United Stares Law or return to the traditional Tribal Court (TTC). The USA court focuses on punishment and harsh treatments. The TTC focuses on restitution, rehabilitation and the return to peace.

The TTC attempts to restore peace and tranquility and to make things right for the victim(s).

To replace anything that has been negatively impacted by the law-breaker.

The Indigenous Nations can be compared to a "Sleeping Giant" because of their recognized Inherent Rights. They can choose any type of government that they want. The Indian Nations can remain as the USA government presently has them with basically no changes and the USA in complete control, what the Indian Nations live under are mainly white man rules, regulations and law.

These Indigenous Nations can remain dependent as the USA government has positioned them

OR

they can be free and independent as any nation on earth with their own rules, regulations and laws

JUDICIAL SYSTEM AND COURTS

Any and all court procedures for the Indians would have to go through the Traditional Tribal Council. Indigenous Nations can perform the functions of any other Sovereign nation, such as issuing;

- vehicles licenses

- Titles

- Permits

- Drivers licenses

- Passports and etc.

- Business licenses which includes all company and corporate licenses.

These Indian Nations would not have to pay taxes of any kind like sales, manufacturing, inventory, import tariff or any other form of taxes, nor would they have to do any type of tax collection for any foreign entity excepting their own government.

The Native Americans own the only corporate entity in this country that can make a profit and not have to pay taxes excepting to their own government. Especially important the individual Native American is not subject to any form of taxes and this includes the IRS.

The Indians can start and operate any kind of business without asking permission from any government or their political sub-divisions excepting from their Traditional Tribal government.

These named privileges are only a small portion of the rights and things that our People will enjoy, but first the Indians must have the right style of government. These named privileges are only a small portion of the Right style of government. These named rights and privileges cannot be enjoyed or practiced under the BIA(Bureau of Indian Affairs)   government controlling everything with the Secretary of Interior having the overriding say.

There is a way that Indian Tribes can get complete control of their Nation is to hold a Special election concerning the Native American government so that they will enjoy their Inherent Rights, to start they must call for this Special Election.

This is how it is done;

- secure the signatures of at least ten percent of your voters of your nation calling for this election

- set a date on the calendar that is at least three weeks into the future,

- state exactly what issues or choices will be put on the ballot,

- select the time and place(s) the voting (polling), will be held,

- the indigenous people of this nation calling for this election for change of government   and officers do not need permission from any entity such as; the United   States government or any of its political subdivisions such as the IRA, the department of interior, or any Indian organization,

- the leaders and officers of the new government must be selected or chosen. Officers and or leaders will be on a temporary basis and they will serve until such a time as the new government is firmly established,

- the new government will take complete control over all the assets and tribal property, all offices, tribal vehicles, equipment, buildings, banking and money etc.

- the new government will closely examine any and all documents, agreements, contracts, bank accounts, all the things that are part of operating a government,

- tribal membership and enrollment is completely up to the elders of the family, clan and tribal elders, - no other permission is needed.

The United Indigenous Nations
Rudy Al James
Secretary-General

- all the following is from law; (a) United Nation laws, (b) some United States Law that endorses UN Law, (c) Tribal Law, (d) Common Law,

- note; some laws from the USA are over 200 years old but those laws are still in effect.

- the Indigenous Peoples and Nations are the only entity that possess the right to be profit   making and being non-taxable.

  (a) We do not have to pay any form of taxes, especially sales taxes, this includes the foreign entities.

  (b) We do not have to pay any income taxes

- the Indigenous Peoples have the recognized right to have their own form of government and their own judicial system.

- The Indigenous Peoples and Nations have the recognized right to have their own courts with their own judges, any and all cases and all charges against an Indigenous person will have to be presented to Indigenous courts, no Indigenous person will have to face double jeopardy.

- An Indigenous person may have multi-citizenships.

PRESENTATION OF CHOICES
Reno, Nevada
TO THE LOCAL INDIGENOUS PEOPLES
Rudy Al James
Secretary-General of the United Indigenous Nations

This Conference is all about Learning the Facts and "Making Choices."

The "present Choice" is to continue to let things go as they have in modern times.

The problems will continue as they are happening now with no evident or apparent long lasting satisfactory solutions, with no good changes in sight.

There are a few good things that happen that often help and benefit certain individuals but they really do not have very good results for everyone.

A lot of Our Rights, Lands and Resources have disappeared from us and have made many of us very unhappy.

Laws and Agreements have been enacted without the permission of all the Tribal Members and those "Laws" have negatively impacted our People.

Laws and Regulations that have been passed **without** the **active participation** of all the **Tribal Members are illegal**!

Or

My Proposed Choice is;

We can and must study the facts, especially about the Laws that affect our Peoples and we must become fully acquainted with what Laws and Agreements that are legal and binding!

There are a number of laws that are in existence and in force that have been enacted for the benefit of Indigenous Peoples and Nations and those laws have been endorsed by the United Nations and the government of the United States of America.

The civilized Nations of the world have all signed and endorsed those laws.

The Full Implementation of all those Laws Will Result in Justice and much Good for all Indigenous Peoples and Nations!

- No Rights, Lands, Waters, Resources can be taken from our People without all the whole tribal membership giving their full agreement.

- A truly Sovereign Nation will have its own Traditional Tribal Court based upon Traditional Tribal Law and using a good portion of International Law.

- Any and all legal actions taken against your Tribal member will have to be filed in the Traditional Tribal Court.

- The Bureau of Indian Affairs directed courts are not a Traditional Tribal Court.

Kuiu Kwaan Court

A Sample Case
A TEST CASE FOLLOWS (NAMES, ADDRESSES AND
PLACES ARE NOT SHOWN.)
Re., Legal Opinion as per your request.

Authority to Disenrollment of a Tribal Membership

This Legal Opinion is based upon Law from *Traditional Tribal Law, United Nations Law and United States Federal Law and Common Law.*

There are probably few things more important than *Tribal membership* or the question of the *disenrollment* of a tribal member.

This legal question or issue must be carefully examined from several perspectives, namely;

- There is a significant difference between being a citizen of a nation or the nationality.

- A person can never lose his or her identity or nationality (his or her race) based on a majority vote of those who control the political power.

- Citizenship maybe acquired by fulfilling certain requirements of a nation, on the other hand, nationality is something acquired by birth and heredity.

- Nations of the world, including Indigenous Nations, have the power to adopt any individual as a citizen or tribal member. Said adoptee would enjoy all the rights of a natural born citizen or tribal member provided that special requirements were met.

- Certain conditions may arise that bring into question of whether or not that some individual(s) personal behavior is detrimental to the welfare of the nation.

- The charge of whether or not to revoke a citizenship must be heard before an unbiased court giving equal time to both parties. That decision should not be made by a political party.

- The accused should be allowed to defend themselves before a neutral court.

- The accusers must present their evidence and accusations at said court.

- The accused will be allowed to present his or her witnesses and evidence as to why their citizenship should not be taken away.

Judgment on Tribal Membership

Rendered by; Thlau Gu Yailth Thlee – The First and Oldest Raven – Lead Judge of the Kuiu Kwaan Court

THE QUESTION AT BAR; Can an Indigenous Tribe dis-enroll or remove the Citizenship or Tribal Membership of a tribal member on a temporary or permanent basis for cause?

Some Fundamentals To Keep In Mind:

- The Goal and Aim of all Tribes is Peace and Tranquility and the

- Complete Protection of All their Tribal Members. Each Tribal Member enjoys his or her Tribal identity.

- There is a fundamental difference between Tribal Identity and Tribal Citizenship.

- Every Tribal Member is born with a Tribal Identity along with Tribal citizenship.

- The Tribal Identity can never be removed.

- The Tribal Citizenship is another matter. Citizenship can be removed, after a formal hearing guaranteeing Personal Rights, for a period of time depending on the seriousness or the infraction of Law or personal conduct.

- The accused have certain rights that have to be considered in his or her case.

- If the tribe is small in number the Council will, of necessity, seek adjudication outside its tribal membership.

- In contemporary society, those who sit in judgment must have an understanding of Traditional Tribal Law, International Law, Common Law and Federal Law.

- One of the most important laws is that "talking behind someone's back" is considered in such a fashion that the only crime that is worse is murder. Those that slander and gossip are viewed as someone who is attempting to destroy the reputation of the person who is being talked or gossiped about.

If the gossip and slander is believed, the person will no longer be viewed and respected as he once was. His stature and standing in his community will be greatly diminished. In the traditional tribal community he will be destroyed or in a very marked way the person that he once was is no longer. That person is gone or destroyed by the slander and gossip. Everyone has to take especial care what he or she says about someone else.

Those that are accused have certain rights by all the various legal entities listed at the first part of this document, namely;

(1) They are to receive a fair and impartial hearing by an unbiased court

(2) They have a right to testify in their own behalf.

(3) They have a right to utilize witnesses.

- If the accused have been found guilty, the eventual "sentence or judgment" concerning the length of time for the removal of "Citizenship" will depend on the seriousness of the infraction of law or code of ethics. The length of the suspension will be determined primarily by the *Tribal Elders*.

- *Restitution and Rehabilitation* are usually an aim. If and when *Restitution* and *Rehabilitation* has been achieved and restored and both sets of Elders are satisfied that peace and tranquility has returned to their society then this incident will never be spoken about again. Those that broke the Law will be given a chance to return completely to their Tribe and live out their life in respectability.

- It must be always remembered that the *Traditional Tribal Societies* were structured in a fashion that honored and respected their *Traditional Tribal Goals and Aims*.

- Where "Forgiveness and Honor" played an important foundational component of the "Ethics of a Tribe", a healthy and vigorous and well respected tribe is in existence.

- *Restitution and Rehabilitation* are a fundamental part of the Judicial Process of a tribal society.

- Only a few crimes, such as murder and violent criminal sexual acts, warrant a tribal member to be completely removed from tribal roles, the circumstances will vary with each case.

The following factual data was utilized to arrive at a decision for the question posed above.

- All Indigenous Tribal Nations have Sovereign Power.

- Said Nations are the equal, politically speaking, of any other nation on earth. Thus, they are the supreme authority over their lands, waters, and resources; including their Tribal Membership.

- The Tribal Elders of the immediate family of said Tribe, are the final authority, with certain exceptions, over their own family members.

- Traditional Tribes have rules and regulations, customs, heritage and etc., all based upon respect and on the personal conduct of said member.

- It is vitally important the proper respect be shown to the tribal leadership. The number of serious crimes is enumerable; every case would have to be heard on its own merits by a neutral panel, court or the respected Tribal Elders. Personal vendettas have no place on such a serious issue.

- All judgments are to breached by a consensus of the Tribunal or panel of judges or the respective panel of family Clan Elders.

- ***"Achieving a consensus,"*** is vital and this is the ***Traditional Way*** to arrive at judgments and decision making.

- The **Traditional Judicial Body** may be composed several ways;

  o It usually is composed of the Respected Tribal or Clan Elders.

  o Some Tribes will have their own Traditional Tribal Court.

  o A "Go Between," a Peacemaker, is very important to the Indigenous judicial system. This position is held by a neutral well-respected man. One of his main functions is to talk with both sides of a legal question to ascertain and make some important determinations regarding the facts of the case.

  o He has to investigate what are the exact problems.

  o He has to identify the principals of both sides of the confrontation and find out what actually took place.

  o He has to meet with both sets of Elders of those involved with the confrontation to arrive at a possible satisfactory solution that involves restitution and restoration of peace and tranquility.

  o Please note that the Principal(s), after they have given their testimony to the *"Peacemaker,"* have almost nothing to do with the process other than confirming the factual information about the infraction of Law.

  o The Peacemaker's efforts are aimed at bringing peace back to their societies.

  o The *Elders* of both sides of the issue will do all the representations, agreements and decision making.

- o If the Peacemaker determines that he cannot achieve a proper solution he then will call to convene the *Traditional Tribal Court (TTC)*, for adjudication.

- o The convening of the TTC brings many more minds to bear on the legal issue. When a "Council of minds" is employed there is much more wisdom.

- o When the terms of the settlement have been satisfactorily met and the infractions of Law are no longer an issue, and

- o When both sets of Elders arrive and reach an agreement with the problem(s) solved, the Peacemaker will convene a PUBLIC Peace Ceremony to notify the society that a satisfactory settlement has been achieved.

- o The Peacemaker will perform a dance ceremony using a headdress that is mounted with white down feathers. As he dances the white down feathers fall softly to the floor signaling that peace has now returned to society.

- o Because there is no longer an issue the Peacemaker makes a Solemn pronouncement and binding declaration; "From now on this issue will never be spoken of again!" It will be like this Infraction of Law never happened and the law-breaker may live his/her life like no infraction of Law took place.

- Depending on the seriousness of one's immoral and or illegal personal conduct, any tribal member can be Banished from his/her Tribal Nation. How long depends on an unbiased Court or the decision of the involved Tribal Elders.

- Where "Forgiveness and Honor" played an important foundational component of the "Ethics of a Tribe", a healthy, vigorous, and well respected tribe is in existence.

The United States of America is signatory to many International Agreements, Treaties and Understandings. Those documents that bear that signature of the USA, become the Supreme Law of the Land (under the Supremacy Clause of the United States Constitution.)

The following Legal Cites pertains to a portion of the laws that identify some of the Inherent Rights of the Indigenous Peoples of North America. These laws obligate the government of the United States of America on how to conduct relations with the Indigenous Peoples. Those governments and their agencies that ignore or do not comply with said laws are subject to prosecution by such laws as P.L. 100-606, the Anti-Genocide Act, and most certainly will be censured by the United Nations.

7 UNITED NATIONS LAW

THE UNITED NATIONS AND HUMAN RIGHT MECHANISM AND PROCEDURES

"The promotion and protection of human rights has been a major preoccupation for the United Nations since 1945, when the Organization's founding nations resolved that the horrors of The Second World War should never be allowed to recur. Respect for human rights and human dignity 'is the foundation of freedom, justice and peace in the world", the General Assemble declared three years later in the Universal Declaration of Human Rights. Over the years, a whole network of human rights instruments and mechanism has been developed to ensure the primacy of human rights and to confront human rights violations wherever they occur.

Protection

"The Centre for Human Rights operates a 24-hour fax "hot line", put at the disposal of victims of human rights violations, their relatives and non-governmental organizations, to allow them to contact the Centre for Human Rights. It also allows the Centre for Human Rights to react rapidly to human rights emergencies."

…UN human rights advisory services and technical assistance.

- Crisis management

- Prevention and early warning

- Assistance to States in periods of transition

- Promotion of substantive rights

United Nations Centre for Human Rights
United Nations Office at Geneva
8-14 Avenue de la Paix
1211 Geneva 10, Switzerland
Tel: 41 22 917 3924
Fax: 41 22 917 0213
New York Liaison Office (CHR)
Room S-2914
United Nations
New York, NY 10017
Fax: (212) 963-4097

Coordination and rationalization of the human rights programme

The Centre for Human Rights in Geneva, part of the United Nations Secretariat, in this connection implements the policies proposed by the High Commissioner.

For further information, please contact: Public Inquiries Unit
Room GA-57
United Nations   Department of Public Information
New York, NY 10017 Tel: (212) 963-5930 Tel. (212)-963-4475

Outline

Business opportunities for Native Americans

- unlike other American business enterprises those businesses belonging to Native American enterprises are completely tax free.

- these tax free enterprises may be located off reservation lands and still be tax exempt.

- the Native American enterprises do not need licenses, permits, zoning regulations or any form of affirmative action from any state or federal entity or their political sub-divisions.

- all the wholesale suppliers that service these Native American enterprises are not allowed to include any form of taxes, i.e., import, manufacturing, inventory, quota systems, shipping or any form of taxes to any item that is sold to the native American retailers.

- the Native American enterprises do not need to give any reports of any kind to any local, state or federal agencies.

Case Law on Sovereign Immunity

In North Sea products versus Clippers Seafood's,
Washington State Supreme Court v. Lummi Nation (Tribe)

92 WN. 2d 236, 590 P.2d 939 (1979), the Superior Court of Whatcom County, Washington issued a writ of garnishment on the Lummi tribe and/or its tribal enterprise which was located off reservation. The Washington Supreme Court stated that the tribe's sovereign immunity from suit includes immunity from garnishment actions. This case recognizing Indian tribes the same immunity from garnishment which other sovereigns possess. The general rule is that the United States and the states cannot be summoned as garnishees without statutory authorization, consent, or waiver from the involved Indigenous Nation.

A CLEAR DECLARATION OF LAW

ANY AND ALL, BUSINESSES WHETHER RETAIL,WHOLESALE, MANUFACTURING, OR ANY TYPE OF BUSINESS ARE NOT SUBJECT TO ANY FORM OF TAXATION AS LONG AS SAID BUSINESS OR ENTERPRISE IS OWNED (BY MAJORITY STOCK) OF NATIVE AMERICANS.

- THE LOCATION OF SAID BUSINESS DOES NOT HAVE TO BE LOCATED ON RESERVE LAND OR TRUST LAND OR USA FEDERAL OR STATE LAND.

The Inherent Rights of the Indigenous People of North America

Please see the United Nations Declaration on the Rights of Indigenous Peoples.

Link   here:
http://www.un.org/esa/socdev/unpfii/documents/DRIPS_en.pdf

The Declaration on the Rights of Indigenous Peoples was adopted by the United Nations General Assembly during its 61st session in New York City on 13 September 2007. President Barack endorsed and the U.S. signed the Declaration on December 16, 2010.

This document is to inform all the nations of the world of certain irrefutable facts concerning indigenous people

This factual data is recognized Traditional Tribal Law – United States Federal Law – United Nations Laws – treaties, accords and understandings

The following Legal Cites pertains to a portion of the laws that identify some of the Inherent Rights of the Indigenous Peoples of North America. These laws obligate all nations of the world, including the government of the United States of America, on how to conduct relations with the Indigenous Peoples. Those agencies of the U.S.A. that ignore or do not comply with said laws are subject to prosecution by such laws as P.L. 100-606, the Anti-Genocide Act, and most certainly will be censured by the United Nations.

Laws between Nations

Foreign Law

"The law of a foreign country, or of a sister state. In conflicts of law, the legal principles of jurisprudence which are part of the law of a sister state or nation. Many states have foreign law provisions in their legal codes that defer to foreign law to prevent manifest injustice," Black's Law Dictionary.

Indigenous law

All of Indian society, culture and all inter-action between Peoples and Nations is predicated on Respect! The Indigenous Peoples and Nations are to treat other Peoples as they would like to be treated. All life is sacred! The Indians are of the opinion that the so-called "wild animals" in Nature are like relatives of theirs. If some of these animals are to be harvested for food, the making of implements, house-hold use etc. they are to be respected and never wasted, in fact much of these animals are to be addressed and told that we apologize for taking their life, however the Creator God has put these animals here for our use.

Comments: There are many more rights available to the Indian Peoples and Nations. The United Nations in Geneva, Switzerland has books published outlining those procedures and rights.

JULY 16, 2013
Winnamucca Nation
Retail
(in the region of Nevada)

This a legal document based on law for operating an indigenous retail unit in America away from any reservation.

Please note that any and all Native American owned and operated retail businesses are not subject to any and all forms of taxation- licenses, and permits, from the USA and its subsidiaries.

"the only business entity that can tax, (and only by agreement), such an operation is its own tribal government." (The USA or any of its political sub-divisions do not have a legal Right to impose any forms of taxation on the Indigenous Peoples and Nations).

Prepared for distribution by the Traditional Tribal Court of The Kuiu Kwaan of Alaska. Lead Judge; Rudy Al James.

Will v. Michigan Department of state police-
Supreme Court ruling reported 1991.

491 US. 58, 57 L W 4677 (1989)

State Officials sued in their individual capacities are "persons" under 42 USC 1983 who may be held liable for damages for civil rights violations. State officials can be held personally liable for actions taken in the course of their official duties. Justice Sandra Day O'Connor wrote thus, section 1983 was designed to redress violation of civil rights by persons acting under the color of state law and thus stood the statute on his head to hold that a state official could not be held liable "precisely because of her authority as a state official."

CONCLUSION

It is abundantly clear that the government of the United States of America considers the Indigenous Nations and Peoples to be a separate People and Nation. Clearly the Indigenous Peoples and Nations are not subject to any form of taxation from any entity, except that of their own. The Indigenous Peoples and Nations have the right to own and operate a business away from their Reservation or "Trust Lands," without business licenses or permits excepting their own. The intention of the Indigenous Peoples and Nations is to own and operate businesses not only on their reservations but also in other areas that are clearly not recognized as Indian Reservations or Trust Lands, all without any form of taxation excepting from their own government!

A CLEAR DECLARATION OF LAW

ANY AND ALL, BUSINESSES WHETHER RETAIL,WHOLESALE, MANUFACTURING, OR ANY TYPE OF BUSINESS ARE NOT SUBJECT TO ANY FORM OF TAXATION AS LONG AS SAID BUSINESS OR ENTERPRISE IS OWNED (BY MAJORITY STOCK) OF NATIVE AMERICANS.

THE LOCATION OF SAID BUSINESS DOES NOT HAVE TO BE LOCATED ON RESERVE LAND OR TRUST LAND OR USA FEDERAL OR STATE LAND.

The United Nations

INTERNATIONAL COVENANT AND POLITICAL RIGHTS
GENERAL ASSEMBLY RESOLUTION 2200A (XX1)

ARTICLE 49
PART 1
ARTICLE 1

- "All people have the right of self-determination. By virtue of that right they freely determine their political status and freely pursue their economic, social and cultural development."

- "…in no case may a people be deprived of its own means of subsistence.

PART 111
ARTICLE 8

- " (A) No one shall be required to perform forced or compulsory labor, …"

ARTICLE 11

- "No one shall be imprisoned merely on the ground of inability to fulfill a   contractual obligation."

ARTICLE 12

- Every one shall be free to leave any country, including his own.

ARTICLE 17

- "No one shall be subjected to arbitrary or unlawful interference with his privacy, family, home or correspondence, nor to unlawful attacks on his honour or reputation."

Convention for the prevention and punishment of the crime of genocide

ARTICLE 1: the contracting parties confirm that genocide, whether committed in time of peace or a time of war, is a crime under international law, which they undertake to prevent and to punish.

ARTCLE 11: in the present convention, genocide means any of the following acts committed with the intent to destroy, in whole or in part, a national, ethnic, racial or religious group, as such.

Declaration of the Rights of persons belonging to national or ethnic, religious or linguistic minorities,

ARTICLE 1

- States shall protect the existence and the national or ethnic, cultural, religious and linguistic identity of minorities within their respective territories and shall encourage conditions for the promotion of that identity.

8 ADDENDUM

The Constitution of the Kuiu Thlingit Nation

Dedicated To the Elders
Who Faithfully
Kept the Oral Tradition Alive
And Transmitted the Precepts of Traditional Tribal Law
To the children of all future Generations
From Whom we are Borrowing this World
Transcribed from the Oral Traditions
of the Kuiu Kwaan Thlingit Nation and the Thleenadih Thlingit
Peoples
of the Region of Southeast Alaska

A Sovereign Nation
Original Holders of Allodial Title

Honoring a Fallen Raven

The Members of the Kuiu Thlingit Nation are deeply indebted to the late Dr. Albert P. Blaustein, Professor Emeritus of Law at Rutgers University School of Law, Camden, New Jersey. Professor Blaustein was one of the world's foremost authorities on the constitutions of the world having served as constitutional counsel for over forty nations, including modern Russia.

Shortly before his untimely death, Dr. Blaustein offered to work with the Kuiu Thlingit Nation, at no financial charge, to draft a constitution.

We honor Dr.Blaustein for the work he did on behalf of so many peoples of the world and we are proud to have called him "friend." With honor and respect, we humbly dedicate this Constitution to his memory.

Preamble

We, the Kuiu Thlingit Nation, Sovereign Peoples under the presence and power of the Great Spirit, the Creator of the Universe, Mother Earth and all life, whose Members have maintained sovereign nationhood since time immemorial, in the exercise of our inherent Sovereignty and inalienable right of self-determination, do hereby bestow unto ourselves and our posterity this Constitution to reaffirm our Great Nation, with the intent to continue as distinct Indigenous Thlingit Peoples, to protect our just rights and liberties, to assert our principles, to achieve genuine social dignity, to affirm our convictions avowing respect for all mankind and all plant, animal, bird and sea life, to proclaim our identity as the Kuiu Thlingit Nation, the Sovereign Nation, Original Holders of Allodial Title, and to promote our aspirations and ideals to all other nations of the world.

We do hereby recognize and respect the inherent, international independence of all Nations, their right and power of regulating their own internal, domestic and international affairs without foreign mandate or dictation. Signatories to this Constitution do forever pledge friendship and support of all Nations and their efforts to perpetuate their unique spiritual, cultural, political and economic self-sufficiency.

Recognizing that our future is found in our past, we reaffirm our inherent right to continue to exist as a distinct People, to maintain and exercise our traditional lifestyle, to live in just, equitable conditions, to preserve and protect our lands, waters and resources, to keep and transmit ancestral territories to future generations in accordance with our Kuiu Nation's publicly defined cultural patterns, social institutions, traditional government and legal systems. We declare that cultures may evolve without altering the fundamental principles of a People's distinct heritage.

We honor and respect our relations and ancestors upon whose lives our lives are built, who established our civilization countless generations ago — a distant time celebrated and remembered in our oral history, sacred ceremonies and traditions, expressed in our artistry, carvings, petroglyphs and the distinctive signs and symbols of our Peoples and culture.

Recognizing that the traditional lands, waters and resources of the Kuiu Thlingit Nation are part of our heritage, integral to our existence and the seats of much Thlingit history and knowledge that are inalienable parts of the world's heritage that add to the cultural and social diversity of mankind, we pledge to honor and protect the unique relationship that exists between our Peoples and Mother Earth.

Be it known that the signatories to this Constitution do hereby claim our right of self-governance, declare that government is legitimate when based upon the consent of the governed and founded upon Traditional Tribal Law. We affirm that government thus grounded should be used to guarantee and enhance life, freedom and the peaceful enjoyment of life, that the individual members of the Kuiu Thlingit Nation have the inalienable right to be free from violations of the integrity of the person to enjoy civil liberties such as freedom of assembly, religion and movement, economic development, physical and social harmony, health and welfare and the freedom to maintain our traditional culture.

The Kuiu Thlingit Nation Members shall exercise the right to utilize our natural resources without interference from any entities or governments. Further, we shall exercise our right to freely trade with the nations of the world and shall conduct foreign relations with those nations that enter into such agreements through time-honored protocols with the exchange of appropriate diplomatic instruments and personnel.

We call upon the nations of the world to honorably and respectably observe the Rule of Natural Law, the provisions of the Charter of the United Nations, the Universal Declaration of Human Rights, the International Covenant on Civil and Political Rights, the Optional Protocol to the International Covenant on Civil and Political Rights, the Declaration on the Rights of Persons Belonging to National or Ethnic Religious and Linguistic Minorities, the Declaration on the Granting of Independence to Colonial Countries and Peoples, General Assembly Resolution GAR 1803 (XVII), "Permanent sovereignty over natural resources," the Convention on the Prevention and Punishment of the Crime of Genocide, the Declaration on the Protection of all Persons from Being Subjected to Torture and Other Cruel, Inhuman or Degrading Treatment or Punishment, the Code of Conduct for Law Enforcement Officials, the Principles of Medical Ethics relevant to the Role of Health Personnel, particularly Physicians, in the Protection of Prisoners and Detainees against Torture and Other Cruel, Inhuman or Degrading Treatment or Punishment, the United Nations Standard Minimum Rules for the Administration of Juvenile Justice (The Beijing Rules), the Convention on the Political Rights of Women, the Declaration of the Rights of the Child, the Declaration on the Protection of Women and Children in Emergency and Armed Conflict, the Declaration on the Right to

Development, the Declaration on the Right of Peoples to Peace, and the Declaration of the Principles of International Cultural Co-operation.

The Kuiu Thiingit Nation calls upon all states and nations to faithfully and strictly respect the Sovereignty of the Kuiu Thiingit Nation as long as there is land and water and as long as the wind blows.

SECTION 1

Constitutional Principles

Article 1 Three fundamental principles that form the foundation of the Kuiu Thiingit Nation are a belief in the Great Spirit, the Creator God, respect for Mother Earth and all her inhabitants and respect for Traditional Tribal Law.

Article 2 Inasmuch as Traditional Tribal Law is based upon the ancient universal moral code as defined by Traditional Tribal Elders and Village Councils, it is a publicly defined legal process in which law and morality are "interconnected and based upon ethics that originated in the acts of will of sovereign Indigenous Lawmakers.

Article 3 Due to the fact that Traditional Tribal Law is a living ,breathing, vital entity, which works for the people, rather than the people working to serve Tribal Law, there is flexibility and creativity in that it can progress to meet the needs of Tribal Members in any age.

Article 4 Traditional Tribal Law obligates Tribal Leaders, Council
Members and Tribal Judges to act in concert with the Leaders of the families and Clans to represent and to protect all Tribal Members, including children, and grandchildren, those yet unborn and all living things. It requires Tribal Leaders to protect their lands, waters and resources for the future seventh generation yet unborn.

Article 5 Traditional Tribal Law incorporates respect, justice, balance, restoration and restitution, which are historically grounded in the unique circumstances and traditional lifestyle of the Kuiu Thiingit Nation.

Article 6 Traditional Tribal Law, as applied by the Kuiu Thiingit Nation, shall at all times be culturally relevant, common sense and practical, with the goal of maintaining balance and harmony.

Article 7 The Kuiu Thiingit Nation is the collective sovereignty of its Indigenous Tribal Members.

Article 8 The Kuiu Thiingit Nation, which holds Allodial Title, shall enjoy all manifestations, embodiments and personifications of inherent sovereignty. The Kuiu Thiingit Nation shall respect, embrace and endorse collective and individual Tribal rights, foster unity among the Tribal Members, while recognizing the value of diversity that is inherent to the sovereignty of the nation.

Article 9 The peoples, lands, waters and resources of the Kuiu Thiingit Nation shall not be subject to taxation by any foreign government or power, nor shall there be any restrictions imposed by any foreign power on the establishment of private businesses, enterprises or joint ventures.

Article 10 The Kuiu Thiingit Nation reserves the right, when and if appropriate, to create systems and programs for material and financial support of its governmental operations and functions.

Article 11 The Kuiu Thiingit Nation is established to serve the needs and aspirations of its Indigenous Peoples. Its fundamental purpose shall be to guarantee their right to continue to exist as distinct Peoples, to protect and actively promote human rights, economic independence, and freedom from exploitation and oppression, utilizing Traditional Tribal Law, the Rule of Natural Law, the Law of Nations and International Law.

Article 12 All citizens are entitled to equal treatment, equal opportunity and protection of their Human Rights. The Kuiu Thiingit Nation shall promote and develop beneficial institutions, programs and services, and shall solicit such development programs as the Tribal Council shall deem appropriate to ensure the achievement of the social dignity of the citizens of the Kuiu Thiingit Nation and the removal of any restraints, barriers and obstacles that impair the full equality of opportunity, equal social treatment and economic self-sufficiency of the membership of the Kuiu Thiingit Nation.

Article 13 This Constitution shall neither diminish nor otherwise impair the inherent Sovereign Immunity of the Kuiu Thiingit Nation. To authorize adversarial suits under Traditional Tribal Law, the Kuiu Thiingit Nation may waive or limit its inherent Sovereign Immunity only by virtue of its laws, enacted pursuant to this Constitution.

Article 14 The Kuiu Thiingit Nation shall honor its Indigenous heritage and shall dedicate itself to the values, customs, traditions and practices of the Nation. All provisions of this Constitution shall be construed and interpreted to protect, enhance and foster the spirituality, culture, traditions, human rights, property rights, lands, waters and resources of the Members of the Kuiu Thiingit Nation.

Article 15 The Kuiu Thiingit Nation shall make every effort to assert and achieve the rights set forth in this Constitution for all their Tribal Members and to that end shall encourage and offer assistance to fellow Indigenous Nations in preparing constitutions setting forth their principles, rights and duties under their Traditional Tribal Law.

SECTION 2

Territory and Jurisdiction

Article 1 The sovereign powers, authority and jurisdiction of the Kuiu Thiingit Nation, which nation owes its sole existence to the tribal membership and their ancestors, who have gone before, shall extend said authority to its citizens and traditional lands, waters and resources.

Article 2 The Kuiu Thiingit Nation holds absolute Allodial Title to its traditional territories, lands, waters and resources as Indigenous People by succession under Traditional Tribal Law. Said Nation has held title to traditional territories from time immemorial and said title antedates any claim of title on the part of any non-Indigenous entities or other civil, political, religious leaders, monarchs or potentates.

Article 3 The claim of "title" to Kuiu Thiingit Nation lands, waters and resources by any entity other than the Kuiu Thiingit Nation, cannot withstand the scrutiny of history and law. No activity of immigrant peoples prejudiced or otherwise extinguished the title of the Kuiu Thiingit Nation to its ancestral lands, waters and resources.

Article 4 Absolute title to lands, waters and resources cannot exist at the same time in different governments or in different nations or in different peoples. Traditional lands, waters and resources are integral to the continuation of the existence and traditional lifestyles of the Kuiu Thiingit Nation. Therefore, the boundaries of the Kuiu Thiingit Nation extend to all of the traditional territories originally held by the Kuiu Thiingit Nation.

Article 5 Under Traditional Tribal Law the Kuiu Thiingit Nation extends its sovereign powers, authority and jurisdiction over its Peoples beyond its geographical boundaries.

Article 6 Under Traditional Tribal Law, the Kuiu Thiingit Nation asserts Personal Jurisdiction wherever its members may reside, Territorial Jurisdiction over traditional lands, waters and resources and Subject Matter Jurisdiction over issues that involve Tribal Members, and Collective Jurisdiction over property and issues of importance to the Kuiu Nation. It is an individual's birth and continuing membership in, or adoption into the Kuiu Thiingit Nation that confirms Personal Jurisdiction in the Tribe over matters that are of concern. Jurisdiction in all matters is exercised pursuant to lineage, kinship, adoption and Traditional Tribal Law and Custom.

Article 7 The Kuiu Thiingit Nation shall devote itself to just and equitable environmental policies over water, resources, land and land use. Policies based upon sustained yield and enhancement shall be the foundation for the utilization of the natural resources.

Article 8 The Kuiu Thiingit Nation shall maintain a culturally relevant management plan honoring the spirituality, lifestyle, traditions and customs of its particular history, ancestry and lineage. Said plan is known as the Coastal Management Plan.

Article 9 The Kuiu Thiingit Nation Sacred . Sites, Environmental Sanctuaries and Zones of Peace shall be set aside and honored according to the Traditions of the Nation. Said sites shall include:

1. Places of religious ceremony and spiritual connection to the Creator;
2. Places of pilgrimage;
3. Sites where the bones of ancestors rest and funeral sites; and
4. Certain other places of historical and cultural significance to be determined by the Kuiu Thiingit Nation.

Article 10 Sacred Sites are uncommon places of peace and tranquility, violence of any kind is forbidden. They must never be defiled by any one and must be protected against vandalism, misuse and abuse, acts of violence, aggression or exploitation. Any and all spiritual or cultural items located at a Sacred Site (drums, rattles, artifacts of any kind) are not to be handled, rifled, touched or removed. All items are to remain as they were when the People placed and left them there.

Article 11 Environmental Sanctuaries are places of uncommon beauty or spiritual significance such as vision quest sites, mountains, buttes, primordial forests or islands where Tribal Members customarily come apart from daily life for renewal of spirit, mind and body.

Article 12 Zones of Peace shall become part of a worldwide movement to nourish cultural heritage and spiritual enlightenment, with a view to preventing any damage or destruction and preserving the rich heritage of mankind. Zones of Peace are never to be used to foster political purposes.

Article 13 No Kuiu Thlingit Nation Member shall engage in activities that will be harmful or detrimental to the environmental quality of another nation.

Article 14 Ultimate consideration shall be given to the respectful relationship between the Kuiu Thlingit Nation and other nations of the world.

SECTION 3

Citizenship

Article 1 Pursuant to its policy of self-determination, the Kuiu Thlingit Nation embraces the principle of self-identification as confirmed by the respective family, Clan, Tribal Historians, Traditional Tribal Council/Elders Council of each Sovereign Indigenous Nation, Original Holders of Allodial Title. The recognition and the composition of Tribal membership rolls are the duties and sole responsibility in perpetuity of each Indigenous Nation according to Traditional Tribal Law. It is an inherent power. No foreign nation, agency or bureau has the right to determine Tribal membership or Tribal Roll.

Article 2 The criteria for the Kuiu Thlingit Nation citizenship may include ancestry, lineage, parentage, location of birth, self-identification, length of residence, adoption, affiliation and community acceptance, as directed and endorsed by the resident Traditional Tribal Council /Elders Council. Citizenship of the Kuiu Thlingit Nation is automatically conferred to all Tribal Members on the Tribal Roll.

Article 3 Citizenship in the Kuiu Thlingit Nation is documented in the Tribal Rolls.

Article 4 The Kuiu Thlingit Nation recognizes that some of its citizens may ascribe to multi-citizenship. A Tribal citizen may simultaneously be a citizen of the Kuiu Thlingit Nation based upon birth, ancestry, lineage and/or adoption and be a citizen of another nation based upon birth, ancestry, lineage and/or adoption. Persons are not required to give up citizenship in other nations to be members of the Kuiu Thlingit Nation. Indeed, Kuiu citizens shall be considered International Citizens and as such be entitled to all of the rights and privileges and Tribal protection appertaining to such citizenship.

Article 5 Pursuant to Traditional Tribal Law no provision on citizenship in this Constitution or in the Law shall have the effect of depriving a citizen of the Kuiu Thlingit Nation of any right, privilege, medical assistance, investments or retirement benefits that derive from another nation, jurisdiction or government.

SECTION 4

Fundamental Rights and Duties

Article 1 The government of the Kuiu Thlingit Nation derives its powers from the consent of its members. The government is established to protect, maintain and execute the collective rights of the tribal members. The government shall not deny any of its citizens the full and equal protection of the law, nor deny or deprive any citizen of his life, liberty or property without strict compliance with the United Nations General Assembly Resolutions, Covenants and Accords and their recognized procedures.

Article 2 The Kuiu Thlingit Nation recognizes, guarantees, promotes and executes the individual and collective rights of its Tribal Members. The Nation is required to faithfully fulfill all its duties and obligations to its citizens.

Article 3 The citizens of the Kuiu Thlingit Nation are entitled to and possess and enjoy without limitation or waiver their inherent and inalienable Human Rights, worth of the human person, respect and fundamental freedoms protected by the Rule of Law and guaranteed by this Constitution.

Article 4 The citizens of the Kuiu Thlingit Nation shall have the right to life, liberty and security of person. They are entitled to and shall possess and enjoy without limitation any and all of the spiritual, human, civil, political, economic, social and cultural rights as set out by Traditional Tribal Law, the International Bill of Human Rights of the United Nations and International Human Rights Covenants and Accords.

Article 5 The citizens of the Kuiu Thlingit Nation shall be entitled to and shall possess and enjoy without limitation or waiver the right to equal protection before Traditional Tribal Law, recognition as persons and any and all of their inherent individual and collective rights as Indigenous Persons and their individual and collective rights as citizens of the Kuiu Thlingit

Nation wherever they may reside, limited only by the respect that must be shown to the host nation.

Article 6 The citizens of the Kuiu Thlingit Nation shall possess and enjoy equal   opportunity   to   participate   in   the   spiritual, cultural educational, economic, subsistence and political resources of the Kuiu Thlingit Nation.

Article 7 All   citizens   of   the   Kuiu   Thlingit   Nation   shall   be free   from   torture,   cruel,   inhuman   or   degrading treatment   or punishment. Any infliction of punishment for crimes worthy of the same will be administered by his/her Traditional Tribal Nation under the terms of the Traditional Tribal Law.

Article 8 The Kuiu Thlingit Nation shall support the right of its citizens:

1.   *To exercise the practice of Spiritual choice based upon belief in the Creator God and custom and Traditional Tribal Law;*
2.   *To educational programs of choice that are congruent and supportive of their long-standing traditions and aspirations;*
3.   *To the right of transfer of past knowledge of their history, culture and traditions in any form of teaching;*
4.   *To the use of their native tongue as the language of first*
   choice in communication;

5.   *To kinship and extended family practices in the traditions and*
   cultural heritage of their clan;
6.   *To   own   and   utilize   their   own   family,   clan, lineage   and traditional*
      geographical site names;
7.   *To know and take pride in who the citizens' ancestors were, including the*
      cultural,   ethnic,   linguistic   and   religious   back ground and interests of their
      particular ancestry;

8.   *To create economic systems and programs based on Traditional Tribal Law and the Rule of Natural Law;*

9.   *To reasonable access and passageway for the utilization of the natural resources.*

Article 9 All Tribal Members shall be free from arbitrary interference and free from false, misleading attacks upon his/her honor and reputation.

Article 10 Every citizen of the Kuiu Thlingit Nation shall possess the right to invoke the judgment of the Traditional Tribal Court.

Article 11 The Traditional Tribal Council may bring a legal question or issue before the International Tribunal, the Supreme Court of the Indigenous Nations, for adjudication if the legal matter is deemed to go beyond the scope of the Traditional Tribal Court of the Kuiu Thlingit Nation.

Article 12 Citizens of the Kuiu Thlingit Nation shall be entitled to effective remedy by the competent tribunal for acts violating the fundamental rights guaranteed by this Constitution and Traditional Tribal Law.

Article 13 Citizens of the Kuiu Thlingit Nation are entitled to full equality to a fair and public hearing by an independent and impartial tribunal in the determination of his/her rights and obligations and of any criminal charge against him/her.

Article 14 All Kuiu Tribal Members have the right to take part in the government of the Kuiu Thlingit Nation by communing with their respective Council Members through their respective Family and/or Clan Elders.

Article 15 All citizens have the right to work, to free choice of employment, just and favorable conditions of work and to protection against unemployment.

Article 16 Everyone has the right to equal compensation for equal work. Citizens who work have the right to just and favorable remuneration ensuring for self and family an existence worthy of human dignity and self-respect, supplemented, if necessary, by traditional social protection.

SECTION 5

Property Rights

Tribal, Moiety and Personal

Article 1 There are thirty-two Thlingit speaking Nations. One-half of the Nations belong to the Raven Moiety and the other half belong to the Eagle Moiety. All Tribes and Clans have property including but not limited to: Traditional Tribal Houses, Tribal regalia, totems, canoes, carvings, furniture, rattles, drums, artifacts and ceremonial costumes that belong exclusively to the collective Moiety membership. The ownership and control rests solely with the family and Clan Elders.. No one of the opposite Tribe is permitted by Traditional Tribal Law to exercise any control over the property of the opposite Moiety.

Article 2 The Peace Regalia of the Official Tribal Peacemaker is to be held in safety, trust and good repair by a Bodyguard of the opposite Tribe or Moiety. It is one of the duties of the Bodyguard to make said regalia available to the Peacemaker whenever there is a need to do so.

Article 3 The Tribal Nations have definite boundaries. All the lands, waters and resources within their respective boundaries belong exclusively to the Tribe. A Tribal member of another Nation cannot utilize the resources without first obtaining permission or a license from the owners of the resource.

Article 4 All citizens have the right to own property alone as well as in association with others.

SECTION 6

Protection and Rights of Women

Article 1 Neglect, abuse and violence against women were never traditional practices among the Indigenous Tribes of the Americas. Such behavior is loathsome and detestable and a grave violation of Traditional Tribal Law. Crimes against women are also crimes against their families, Clans and Tribes.

Crimes against women threaten the stability of families, negatively impact children and compromise the wellbeing of the Tribe. Abuse of women portends misfortune, depravation and disaster and threatens the very ability of a Tribal Nation to continue.

Article 2 Women of the Clan, village or Tribe enjoy broad personal and property rights, powers, privileges and protections on equal terms with men, without discrimination. Said rights are protected under this Constitution.

Article 3 Women are entitled to live in the spirit of peace, justice, freedom, dignity, mutual respect and understanding, enjoy the fruits of social and cultural progress and may on their part contribute equally to same.

Article 4 Women in all circumstances are among the first to receive protection and relief.

Article 5 Women shall be protected against all forms of neglect, and cruelty.

Article 6 Women are not to be the subjects of traffic or exploitation, in any form.

Article 7 The ability to carry life is an honored and sacred responsibility. A mother's welfare, disposition and state of mind and spirit are crucial for the healthy state of the new life. The mother has a responsibility to conduct her life with care during her term and the family, Clan and Tribal members must treat her and the new child with honor, love and respect.

Article 8 The Kuiu Thlingit Nation has the duty to extend particular care to widows without a family and to those without adequate means of support. Widows shall receive   special care and concern and are entitled to a secure place in which to live and to share in the first fruits of harvests, hunts and production of the Tribe.

Article 9 Single Mothers of children and women without partners do not stand alone. They shall receive special protection and concern and are entitled to safe places in which to live and are guaranteed the opportunity to be productive, contributing members of the Tribe and are allowed to share in the harvests, hunts and production of the Tribe.

Article 10 The Kuiu Thlingit Nation shall support the time honored method of administering justice through the Women's Tribunal regarding sexual crimes against women and their daughter(s). The female relations of an alleged victim form the legitimate court to determine the innocence or guilt of someone charged with a sexual crime against a woman or female child.

Article 11 At an appropriate time, determined by the family Elders of the opposite Moiety, a widow or widower may be the subject of having a marriage arranged so that no one may have to live a life of loneliness.

Article 12   The widows must have a man to be the husband to provide the necessities of life. The age of the man may vary, from a young man to a mature man, regardless of the age of the widow. The arrangement for a widower is on the same basis.

Article 13 The replacement partner automatically inherits the deceased mate's property.

SECTION 7

Rights and Protection of Children and Youth

Article 1 Children and youth are the most vital resources to the continued existence of Indigenous Peoples and to the continuation of the integrity of the culture and society. From the time life first begins, the child is considered a human being and a Tribal member with an identity. They enjoy "person-hood" and full respect.

Article 2 Unborn children can hear in the womb and have the ability to absorb wisdom and knowledge and bond with family members in the prenatal state. An elevated climate of positive expectations for the child is essential within the surrounding family and Clan environment. At the moment of birth children are considered to be as close to the Creator as they can be until their walk on this earth is completed. Therefore, children must be nurtured with love, respect and great care.

Article 3 Children and youth, regardless of age or gender, are entitled to and guaranteed all the rights, powers, privileges and protections available to them on the same basis as those enjoyed by adults under the Traditional Tribal Laws of the Kuiu Nation.

Article 4 Children of tender years shall not, save in exceptional circumstances to be determined by Tribal authorities and/or Tribal judges, be separated from their mothers. If separation is to occur, the child's Indigenous maternal family and Clan shall be among the first considered for alternative placement. All due care and regard must be given to the cultural, linguistic and religious background and interests of their particular ancestry. Parenthood is a lifetime commitment and parents, children, families and Clans shall deal constructively with one another in the best interests of the children, family, Clan and Tribe.

Article 5 Children and youth shall be protected against all forms of neglect, cruelty and exploitation and are not to be the subject of traffic in any form.

Article 6 Children and youth shall in no case be caused or permitted to engage in any occupation or employment that would prejudice their health or education, or interfere with their spiritual, cultural, physical, mental or moral development.

Article 7 Children and youth in all circumstances shall be among the first to receive protection, sustenance, adequate housing, cultural training, education and relief.

Article 8 Special and specific care must be extended to children and youth without an immediate family and to those without adequate means of support. There are no orphans in Traditional Indigenous society. The nearest responsible next of kin have to step forward to assume the role of parents.

Article 9 Children and youth are not property and cannot be given over or sold.

Children who have been adopted out of culture shall retain their rights to citizenship in the Kuiu Thlingit Nation, as with all their children and their children's children.

Article 10 Children and youth have the right to a safe place to live.

Article 11 No child or youth of an Indigenous Nation may be deprived of his or her name, family, Clan or lineage. They have the right to know and take pride in who they are and who their ancestors were.

Article 12 Indigenous Courts have exclusive original jurisdiction, with respect to matters involving Indigenous Children and youth, subject only to competent parents and responsible relatives without waiver or limitation.

Article 13 Mothers and Fathers of Indigenous children and youth have the benefit of the absolute right to revoke consent to relinquishment of their children.

Article 14 Mentally or physically handicapped children and youth shall, whenever possible, live with their families or Clans and participate in different aspects of community life. The families with which they live shall receive assistance, if that is necessary. Every attempt shall be made to provide surroundings as close as possible to those of normal life, if care in an institution becomes necessary. Mentally or physically handicapped children have the right to be declared wards of the Tribal Court, when this is required to protect their interests and personal wellbeing.

SECTION 8

Marriage

Article 1 No marriage shall be legally entered into without the full and free consent of both parties, such consent to be expressed by them in person in the presence of the Tribal authority competent to solemnize the marriage. Marriage by proxy is permitted only when the competent Tribal authority is satisfied that each party has fully and freely expressed consent before witnesses and not withdrawn such consent.

Article 2 No marriage shall be legally entered into by any person under the age of 20 except where a competent Tribal authority has granted a dispensation as to age.

Article 3 Men and women of full age have the right to marry and to found a family. They are entitled to equal rights as to marriage, during marriage and at its dissolution. The family is the natural and fundamental unit of Tribal society and is entitled to protection by the Tribe.

Article 4 The Elders of both the woman and the man are expected to give advice and instructions to the newlyweds and inform them of their duties and obligations to each other and to the union of the two Tribes. Each spouse shall be informed as to how they must show respect and conduct themselves toward one other as this behavior is an exact measure of how they respect and honor the opposite family, Clan and Tribe. Both sets of Elders shall make it abundantly clear to the newlyweds that the marriage is more than two people exchanging vows to join their paths through this life. The marriage also symbolizes a joining together of two opposite Moieties.

Article 5 As per Traditional Tribal Law, no marriages are permitted between close blood or members or of the same Moiety.

SECTION 9

The Kuiu Thlingit Nation National Government
Based Upon Traditional Tribal Law

Article 1 The Traditional Tribal Council is the supreme governing body.

Article 2 The Traditional Tribal Council is composed of representatives of Clans (a large grouping of families). The Tribal Council Members are selected by their respective Clan Elders, who have joined together for the common good based on the Constitution of the Kuiu Thlingit Nation

Article 3 The Traditional Tribal Council, in convention assembled, reserves all powers of government unto itself and its designees.

Article 4 The appointment of each Tribal Council Member is an exclusive Function of the Traditional Clan Council/Tribal Elders Council. These said Clan Councils are the only entities that possess the authority to appoint their own Representatives or to remove said individual(s) from the Traditional Tribal Council.

Article 5 The length of the term of the Tribal Council Member is determined exclusively by the respective Traditional Clan Council/Elders Council, based upon competent service.

Article 6 Each Council member serves at the pleasure of his/her
Traditional Clan Council/Elders Council. Said Representative(s) carry the honor, name and respect of the Clan Elders that sent him/her.

Article 7 The Traditional Council Member is bound by Traditional Tribal Law to conduct him/herself on the highest personal level while participating in conducting the affairs of state in the General Assembly. There will be no actions for personal gain or self-aggrandizement The first and highest loyalty will be to properly represent the interests of the People of his/her respective Clan.

Article 8 Duties of the Traditional Tribal Council

1.   All the powers of government, the Legislative, the Judicial and the Executive Branch of the Kuiu Thlingit Nation are vested in the Traditional Tribal Council Assembled and have the power, duty and responsibility to   provide laws, ordinances and resolutions to:

1.1 Govern the conduct of Kuiu citizens;

1.2 Regulate the land and resources of the Kuiu Thlingit Nation including the right to
(1) acquire lands and Resources;
(2)   the right to prevent the sale, disposition, lease, use or encumbrance of lands and resources when injurious to the interests of the Kuiu Nation;
(3) the right to otherwise enter into agreement to lease or grant the use of lands and resources to private persons and public bodies; and
(4) the right to provide for the proper use and development of Kuiu lands and resources;

1.3 To manage, protect, preserve and regulate hunting, fishing and fowling rights in the Kuiu Thlingit Nation;

1.4 To monitor all activities which might have an environmental impact and take action to ensure proper environmental protection.

1.5 To levy assessments and collect taxes, both directly and indirectly;

1.6 To approve, adopt and amend annual budgets and to authorize the expenditure of funds in accordance with those budgets;

1.7   To regulate finance and economic development and trade, both with the Nation and with foreign nations and international organizations;

1.8 To regulate inheritance of personal property and interests in lands;

1.9   To provide for the maintenance of law and order, the administration of justice and the preservation of Kuiu Kwaan customary   law by establishing judicial tribunals, law enforcement agencies and criminal and civil laws necessary to the governance of the Kuiu Thlingit Nation;

1.10 To provide for educational, cultural and social institutions and other
    measures for the preservation of the Thlingit language, culture and
    traditions;

1.11 To promote, protect and provide for the social wellbeing of the Kuiu Peoples with measures   (1) on   domestic   affairs   to strengthen the family unit and the traditions of the extended family and Clan relationships; (2) on adoption and appointment of guardians for minor and incapacitated persons; (3) on public health generally and especially for the health and care of elders; and (4) on housing;

1.12   To approve appointments by consensus and retain professional
and technical advisors;

1.13   To enact laws, ordinances and regulations necessary and proper to   carry out the foregoing powers   and   such   other legislative responsibilities   incumbent upon the Tribal Council assembled pursuant to this Constitution.

2. The Traditional Tribal Council shall select the Tribal Leader by consensus who will be known as the President of the

Kuiu Thlingit Nation and shall serve as the official representative of the Kuiu Thlingit Nation. The President shall oversee, implement and execute all laws, ordinances and resolutions enacted by the Tribal Council and shall serve as long as he enjoys the respect and confidence of the Tribal Council. The President may call the Tribal Council into special session.

3. In the event of death, resignation or other inability to discharge his duties as President of the Kuiu Thlingit Nation, the President shall be replaced by the Secretary of State or Gowukaan until such time as the Tribal Council can select a suitable replacement.

4. The Traditional Tribal Council shall by consensus select the Tribal leader -Kaan Koonai (President), Tribal Spokesman, Gowukaan -Peacemaker (Secretary of State), Naa Klaa - Clan Mother (Minister of Domestic Affairs), Lead Judge, Minister of Finance, Minister of the National Treasury, Minister of Education, Minister of Health, Minister of Economic Trade and Development.

5. Ambassadors, High Commissioners, Charges d'Affaires, Consuls, Trade Commissioners and other Diplomatic Officers shall be appointed by consensus by the Tribal Council to represent the Kuiu Thlingit Nation in embassies and consulates to be established in many parts of the world including but not limited to the United States, Canada, other Indian Nations and in nations beyond said borders. Diplomatic representatives shall also be designated to Indigenous organizations. Representatives shall be sent to conferences and meetings of the United Nations and other international organizations dealing with issues relating to human rights, Indigenous rights, minority rights, environmental protection and other issues deemed appropriate by the Tribal Council.

6. In Assembly and by consensus the Traditional Council shall empower and staff the following listed Councils and Commissions and other commissions that may be necessary to carry out the objectives and goals of this Constitution:

The following is a diagram of some of the national offices; every nation will have some variation of this diagram;

Councils and Commissions

FOREIGN RELATIONS COUNCIL	DOMESTIC COUNCIL
PEACE KEEPERS and	COUNCIL ON TRIBAL LAW
PROTECTION COUNCIL	JUDICIAL and NATIONAL TRIBUNAL
TREASURY COUNCIL	HEALTH and MEDICINE COUNCIL
REVENUE COUNCIL	EDUCATION COUNCIL
ECONOMIC, TRADE and COMMERCE COUNCIL	CULTURAL and HERITAGE COUNCIL
NATURAL RESOURCES COUNCIL Forestry, Minerals, Fisheries, Land, and Petroleum	SCIENCE, TECHNOLOGY and INDUSTRIAL COUNCIL
AGRICUTURE and AQUACUTURE	TRANSPORTATION COUNCIL
ENVIRONMENTAL COUNCIL	

- The Tribal Council is empowered to retain legal counsel, accountants and other professional and technical advisors.

Article 9 The Members of the Kuiu Thlingit Nation Judiciary shall be chosen by consensus by the body of the Tribal Council. The Judiciary shall initially consist of six judges with the Tribal Council empowered to increase the number of judges upon request of the Chief Judge or other Members of the Tribal Council. The Kuiu Judiciary shall select a Chief Judge by consensus from among their membership who shall serve as Chief administrative officer. Each member shall perform the duties of a trial judge.

Article 10 The Kuiu Thlingit Nation Judiciary shall have the power to interpret, construe and apply the Traditional Tribal Laws of the Nation. The Judiciary is further empowered to issue injunctions and attachments and writs of mandamus and habeas corpus.

Article 11 Other Nations may call upon the Kuiu Thlingit Nation Court to serve as a surrogate court by formal request through the exchange of diplomatic letters.

SECTION 10

Diplomacy and Foreign Affairs

Article 1 Unless otherwise provided in this Constitution, any agreement between other Sovereigns (including other Indigenous Nations and Nations of the World) and the Kuiu Thlingit Nation shall have the form and the substance of an international treaty. It shall adhere to its worldview of the terms and obligations of its treaties of peace and friendship.

Article 2 The Kuiu Thlingit Nation and its members shall not interfere with the affairs of another Tribal Nation nor shall its citizens fish, hunt or utilize the resources or assets of another Tribal Nation without the consent of the owners of the affected territories.

Article 3 The Kuiu Thlingit Nation and its citizens shall respect the geographical boundaries of each Tribal Nation honoring and observing traditional nation-to-nation etiquette and protocols.

Article 4 International conflicts shall be resolved under the mediation of the appropriate Peacemaker and the respective Tribal Councils and/or the International Tribunal.

Article 5 Other Tribal Nations shall enjoy the right to call upon the bonds of brotherhood, language and kinship that exist between the First Nations of the World and to exercise their right to Send the Feather (or other traditional sign or symbol for requesting assistance), and to request help from the Kuiu Thlingit Nation in mediation and conflict resolution.

SECTION 11

Compacts, Treaties and Constructive Agreements

Article 1 The Government of the Kuiu Thlingit Nation will enter into Compacts, Treaties and other Constructive Agreements with Indigenous Nations and Peoples and with other Members of the World Family of Nations for mutual interests and benefits which include but are not limited to:

1. Protection of Human Rights

2. Humanitarian Outreach

3. Protection of Natural Resources

4. Protection of Endangered Species

5. Habitat Reclamation, Restoration, and Enhancement

6. Establishment of Trading and Economic Networks

7. Establishment of Central Bank, Banking System and Chartering of other Banks

8. Development of New Technology

9. Assist in the return of Human Remains and associated funerary objects known to have been removed from Traditional Indigenous Lands

10. Safeguard Sacred Sites and Environmental Enclaves

Article 2 The Kuiu Thlingit Nation encourages peaceful cooperation and coordination with nations whose territories border and abut the Indigenous Nation.

Article 3 The President of the Kuiu Thlingit Nation, the Secretary   of State, the Minister of Finance and other duly designated Tribal Representatives   may   enter into Negotiations, Treaties and Agreements on behalf of the Kuiu Thlingit Nation, said agreements being subject to ratification by the Tribal Council.

SECTION 12

Ratification and Amendments

Article 1 This Constitution shall come into effect following consensus and ratification by the Tribal Council representing the wishes of the citizens of the Kuiu Thlingit Nation.

Article 2 Amendments to this Constitution shall require a full consensus of the Tribal Council.

Article 3 This Constitution honors the Spirituality, Culture, History, Oral Traditions, Life Style, Lands, Waters and Resources of the Kuiu Thlingit Peoples and all that the Kuiu Peoples Hold Sacred.

Thlau Goo Yailth Thlee, Rudy James

- *The First and Oldest Raven*
- *Spokesman For the Kuiu Kwaan Council*
- *Secretary-General of the United Indigenous Nations*
- *Member of the Board of Governors of the International Human Rights Association of American Minorities (A United Nations NGO with Roster Status)*
- *Lead Judge of the Kuiu Kwaan Traditional Court*
- *A visiting judge for many Indigenous Nations*

Terms and Conditions

<u>LEGAL NOTICE</u>

The Publisher has strived to be as accurate and complete as possible in the creation of this work, notwithstanding the fact that he does not warrant or represent at any time that the contents within are accurate due to the rapidly changing nature of the Internet.

While all attempts have been made to verify the information provided in this publication, the Publisher assumes no responsibility for errors, omissions, or contrary interpretation of the subject matter within. Any perceived slights of specific persons, peoples, or organizations are unintentional.

In practical advice books, like anything else in life, there are no guarantees made. Readers are cautioned to rely on their judgment about their individual circumstances and to act accordingly.